Coloring Book
about
L E N T

Text by MICHAEL GOODE
Illustrations by MARGARET A. BUONO

CATHOLIC BOOK PUBLISHING CO.
NEW YORK

LENT — Season of Preparation for Easter

Lent is a period of forty days in preparation for Easter. We pray, fast, and do good works in imitation of Christ's example.

(T-697)

NIHIL OBSTAT: Francis J. McAree, S.T.D.
Censor Librorum

IMPRIMATUR: ✠ Patrick J. Sheridan, D.D.
Vicar General, Archdiocese of New York

LENT — Time to Gain God's Grace

Lent is a wonderful time for us to gain the grace of God. It offers us many ways in which we can become better persons.

LENTEN SYMBOLS
Ashes

On Ash Wednesday, the first day of Lent, we go to church. The priest makes the Sign of the Cross with ashes on our foreheads.

Ashes are a symbol that we are not made only for this life on earth. Our true home is in heaven with Jesus.

LENTEN SYMBOLS
Fasting

The Church asks us to fast from meat on Ash Wednesday and the Fridays of Lent. In this way we show respect and love for Christ Who died for us on Friday.

We give up certain things we like to do or certain foods we like to eat. In this way, we thank Jesus for all He has done for us.

LENTEN SYMBOLS
The Color Purple

During this time, the priest wears purple vestments at Mass. Other objects in church are also clothed in purple.

Purple is a color that stands for penance. It tells us that we should ask God to forgive any wrong we have done.

LENTEN SYMBOLS
Palm Branches

The sixth Sunday of Lent is called Palm Sunday. We hold blessed palm branches in our hands as the Passion of Christ is proclaimed at Mass. Then we take them home with us.

Palms stand for victory over sin and death. With them, we praise Christ, the King of Kings.

LENTEN PEOPLE
The Patriarch Abraham

Abraham believed God's promise to him. He became the father of all believers.

During Lent, we should put our trust in God. No matter what happens we can always put our faith in Jesus.

LENTEN PEOPLE
The Apostle Paul

St. Paul tells us that Lent is the time of salvation. It is the time that God gives great grace to all.

During Lent, we should be especially careful to be pleasing to God. We should do everything for Jesus.

LENTEN PEOPLE
The Samaritan Woman

The Samaritan Woman spoke with Jesus at the well. Then
she became His follower and spread the Good News to others.

During Lent, we should be more devoted followers of Jesus. We should also pray that all people may follow Him.

17

LENTEN PEOPLE
The Man Born Blind

The Man Born Blind received his sight from Jesus, Light of the World. Then he went out and spread the Good News to others.

During Lent, we should ask Jesus to give light to our minds. We should try to learn more about the Catholic Faith.

LENTEN PEOPLE
Lazarus

Lazarus was brought back to life by Jesus. He praised Jesus and spread the Good News to others.

Jesus has given us the life of grace that leads to heaven. We should ask Him to give that life to all people.

LENTEN PEOPLE
The Children of Jerusalem

The Children of Jerusalem praised Jesus as He entered their city in triumph. They shouted: "Hosanna in the highest."

During Lent, we should praise Jesus, our Lord. We should ask Him to take care of the children of the whole world and give our pennies to the missions.

23

LENTEN DEVOTIONS
Going to Confession

Jesus has left us the Sacrament of Penance. By confessing our sins, we receive forgiveness and grace.

Jesus has given us the Sacrament of the Eucharist. We receive the Body and Blood, Soul and Divinity of Jesus under the signs of bread and wine.

Jesus has given us the Holy Sacrifice of the Mass. It is the living Memorial of the Passion, Death, and Resurrection of Jesus. We should participate at Mass every Sunday.

During Lent, we should try to participate at some Weekday Masses, if possible. We give glory to God and obtain grace for eternal salvation.

LENTEN DEVOTIONS
The Way of the Cross

The Way of the Cross is a devotion in which we follow Jesus during His Passion and Death. It helps us apply the graces of Christ's sufferings to our lives.

During Lent, we should think often of all that Jesus suffered for us. We can then offer our prayers and works to help children all over the world.

LENTEN DEVOTIONS
Visits to the Blessed Sacrament

Jesus is present in the Tabernacle under the sign of the Host that is kept to bring Communion to the sick and the dying.

During Lent, we should make short visits to Jesus in the Blessed Sacrament. We should adore Him as our Lord and God and ask His help to make a good Lent.

PRAISING GOD

During Lent, we thank God the Father for creating us, God the Son for redeeming us, and God the Holy Spirit for making us holy.